MISSOURI

MISSOURI

PHOTOGRAPHY BY OLIVER SCHUCHARD
TEXT BY JOHN M. HALL

GRAPHIC ARTS CENTER PUBLISHING COMPANY,
PORTLAND, OREGON

To Judy
whose support, hard work and
encouragement has made it all possible.
—Oliver Schuchard

International Standard Book Number 0-912856-76-9
Library of Congress Card Number 81-86039
Copyright© 1982 by Graphic Arts Center Publishing Company
P.O. Box 10306 • Portland, Oregon 97210 • 503/224-7777
Designer • Robert Reynolds
Typesetter • Paul O. Giesey/Adcrafters
Printer • Graphic Arts Center
Bindery • Lincoln & Allen
Printed in the United States of America

Page ii: Twelve of the fourteen tribes of
grasses found in North America are
native Missouri flora. Here Nodding
Foxtail grows on native prairie.

Page 5: Deep in the forest of twelve
thousand acres that is the Hercules
Glades Wilderness Area in Taney
County, you can hear the sounds of
many creatures and many winds.

Above: When rivers cut into igneous rock, they form "shut-ins" like this one on the St. Francis River at Silver Mines eight miles west of Fredericktown. *Left:* Roaring River Spring in Barry County south of Cassville provides water for one of Missouri's largest trout hatcheries. *Overleaf:* The Eleven Point River, one of the Ozark National Scenic Riverways, flows through the Irish Wilderness.

Above: The sight and fragrance of wild trees burst into Missouri spring: dogwood, hawthorn, black cherry, and this wild plum, all with white blossoms, all with their own beauty. *Right:* Wild sweet William peeks up from the low canopy of May-apples blooming with flowering dogwood in dense forest north of Westphalia.

Above: Winter brings a magic light to the tall pines in the Cedar Creek Ranger District of the Mark Twain National Forest near Guthrie. *Left:* Missouri prairies become a sea of greening grasses in early spring, enriching the dirt brought by centuries of winds to this Old Plains region along the Missouri-Kansas border.

Above: The rugged hills of the Cedar Creek Ranger District blend into creek valleys, providing a haven for wildlife. *Right:* The broad-leafed jewel weed and the flowering *Hydrophyllum* or waterleaf bloom in Huckleberry Ridge State Forest in McDonald County. *Overleaf:* Sunset silhouettes a cypress in the Mingo National Wildlife Refuge, containing the state's largest natural lake.

MISSOURI

The story of Missouri begins with the wind and the waters. Missouri is an ancient place, as old as the beginning of Earth, 4.6 billion years ago. Sharks swam the ocean over sea flowers blooming in this early time. Evidence of their passing can be found in the sedimentary layering of limestone that forms Missouri hills.

When the seas receded, geophysicists believe, the continents were one. Riding on the molten sea beneath us, the one continent broke into two as the seas filled in around them. Eventually the North American continent broke away on its own journey through time.

The Missouri Ozarks rose out of receding ocean waters 500 million years ago. Together with the Appalachian and Mexican plateaus, the Ozark plateau is the oldest land form on the North American continent. The Rocky Mountains rose to their majesty a mere 125 million years ago.

If you could hear the lichen and the moss in the quiet valleys of the Ozark forest, you would hear the stories of 500 million years. Part of Missouri is that old. As you drive the highways, think of time measured in the layers of limestone. Consider the reach of Missouri's years.

One hundred and forty million years ago, the waters of the Gulf of Mexico lapped against the shores of the Missouri Bootheel. Dinosaurs trudged through the cypress swamps of southeast Missouri. Streams flowed deep in Missouri soil to the granite floor of Missouri's Shut-Ins in the valley of the St. Francois Mountains. The granite, fired in the intense heat of volcanoes, is as old as the granite on the floor of the Grand Canyon and the same elevation.

Life in Missouri is full of the subtle differences to be found where prairie meets the hill country that reaches toward the southeastern lowlands and north to rich farm lands. Follow the geologic flow across the topographical map of the United States into Missouri and you can see the flow of vastly different parts of America traveling toward the confluence of the Missouri with the Mississippi River. Much of the force that is Missouri has to do with the way one part blends into another as hills meld into valleys and valleys run with water in the rain, reaching for the rivers.

The diversity of this place occurs along every geological and biological edge and must be numbered as one would count the beauty and diversity of wildflowers and butterflies. There is an island in the Mississippi River near Hannibal, Jackson's Island, where Tom and Huck and Jim hid out in the stories of Mark Twain. An Audubon Society census recorded 250 species of birds living on this one island.

Think of the colors in the sky as the birds of Missouri travel through their migrations. Each winter eagles fly south to feed in the open waters of the Missouri and the Mississippi rivers. Each spring and each fall the birds and the butterflies migrate through this place. We are part of the wildflowers of a summer day and the stars of a winter night.

* * * * *

Mark Twain said: "I was a traveler! A word never tasted so good in my mouth before." Other travelers have passed through Missouri, forming part of the vision that has become their life. Travelers like Twain were changed by the winds and the rivers of Missouri. Every morning young Samuel Clemens came out of his boyhood home in Hannibal, looking left down the street to the Mississippi River. What boy could resist the power and the mystery and the adventure of such a river? How can we resist its power today? It is not enough to say we are no longer boys.

Out on the river learning to be a river pilot, Twain wrote: "The face of the water, in time, became a wonderful book— a book that was a dead language to the uneducated passenger, but which told its mind to me without reserve, delivering its most cherished secrets as clearly as if it uttered them with a voice. And it was not a book to be read once and thrown aside, for it had a new story to tell every day." By the time Twain knew the river well enough to navigate day or night, the romance was gone and he left for other places. Whether we yield to the river as completely as Twain did, or whether we stand with our children on the banks, the rivers of Missouri are a force in our lives, always changing, always the same.

In Missouri, rivers are as much a part of the story as the weather. Our winters and our summers make us strong. In this story we will consider the continuous flow of waters and winds. We will walk in the Irish Wilderness until we come upon three eagles. We will float in the quiet of an Ozark stream. We will walk in a glade. We will consider the vision arising from our cities, and the quiet beauty of small towns where you can hear the sound of a screen door opening into morning and the porch swings of evening. We will consider the mixing of one civilization with another as the tribes of the white man's nation mix their footprints on the trails of the Indian nation before us. We will watch the river valleys fill with farms as the music of the Scotch-Irish fills the hill country. They bale cotton in the southeast and hang tobacco to dry in northwest Missouri, and pause at the end of each day for a little night music from the stars.

* * * * *

RIVERS AND STREAMS

"Behold these rushing waters
I have not made them without a purpose
I have made them to be the means of reaching
old age."

from an Osage Indian ritual

The magic of an Ozark stream begins in the quiet. The river flows, and the boat moves along under the trees as morning fog rises through the limbs of oak and beyond the reach of mottled sycamore. Soon the frost will come in that final rush and leaf snap as the cycle of life turns into the final hours of autumn.

The river we have come to float this day is near the beginning of our journey. The stream is narrow and swift, confident and strong. The trees move as the clouds move. The creatures along the river go about their lives: deer slipping away from water's edge as the boat rounds another bend; the little blue heron moving just beyond the deer to wait in the shallows for its first catch.

The boatman, alert but easy, sits from standing. He knows the water is deep enough. There are no snags. He adjusts the stern slightly as the boat floats through. Water slaps the sides as he turns the bow into the current again, moving quickly through the shallows into the long still pool beyond. A smallmouth bass strikes the surface in the shadow of an ancient sycamore. The bass breaks water, trying to shake free of the hook. All concerns beyond the moment are gone.

Everything that lives can be seen as the river cuts through the life of animal and man. Those who listen begin to see: the gray squirrel watching; the kingfisher perching; the pileated woodpecker crossing the river in one swoop followed by its mate, holding to the trunk of a sycamore, then dropping with one glide into the dense growth of trees beyond the bank on the other side of the river.

What goes on here that we do not see, that man has forgotten how to perceive? The river opens our ears and our eyes. The color of another indigo bunting is loud enough to be a sound. The river moves through another bend, laughing. The day passes in such a way that morning fog is now evening haze settling in the valley with the first sound of an

owl, and the promise of a moon rising where the sun used to be.

The chuck-will's-widow swoops the water, a dark shape many times the size of the nimble bats who fly their feeding flight, their wings like the sweep of quick and random hands gathering up the last light of day.

In the quiet, you have become one with the river and the trees and the light from the stars. Darkness holds this cargo of souls floating with the boat. On such a night you can hear forever in the valley of silence where the river is flowing.

* * * * *

FLOATING

He went out in the last light of night, across the porch where I was sleeping in this primitive cabin, way the hell and gone back up in the hills of Shannon County. I heard him for the first time when he came in with the squirrel. When I crawled out of my sleeping bag, Red had the meat frying in a cast-iron skillet.

Fog held to the river as we waited for fried squirrel, biscuits, and gravy. The men all took a pull on the whiskey bottle before and after breakfast. Then we headed for the boats.

The talk of river men is basic: "I'll bet you a full dollar to a dried apple," Red said to his brother Jessie, "I catch more fish 'n you do." He pushed the john boat into the current, casting across his paddle arm for the first strike of the day.

We had come down late the night before to this hill cabin where these two bachelors lived on wild game, biscuits, gravy, and whiskey. They were river guides when they wanted to be, and characters all the time. I was just a kid out with his dad and some friends for a float on the Current River.

Red and Jesse Chilton were hill boys and knew the rivers and the forest, and more, from a lifetime of living there. You might come to understand everything you'd ever need to know if you floated rivers long enough.

You come to understand a different kind of humor on the river. Men running boats for hire don't often say any more than they have to, and often they speak in ways that make a few words count for a lot.

When spinning rods first hit the market, my father bought one with a new reel. After his first wild cast of a Lazy Ike into the trees, the guide said, "Larry, fish come down out of the trees when the dew is off." Humor just as dry as the bottom

Fed by an average daily flow (from Big Spring) of 277 million gallons, Big Spring Creek flows into the Current River near Van Buren.

of the john boat, a point of pride with river guides I know.

River men take pride in such things as sassafras paddles, but you won't find sassafras paddles these days any easier than you'll run across characters like Red and Jesse Chilton on the Current, or George Foster on the James before it was dammed, or Bland Wilson and Paul Holley on the Big Piney. Paul always kept sassafras paddles.

Now let's float a ways. The john boat is loaded, the rods are all strung, and we're ready to push off. I got me a 50-foot nylon rope tied to the left back handle on the stern of the john boat, the "ass-end" they say in the hills. A river guide taught me a rope was the best way to lead your boat through a tricky place you weren't sure how to run. That lesson is part of the reason I've never turned one over in Missouri rivers. These rivers are beautiful because they run fast, which is why running a river is fun.

The first white men to float Ozark streams were explorers and fur trappers. Canoes did the job for them. But when settlements took hold, loads heavier than furs required the high-sided, flat-bottomed, full-bellied, square-end john boats. Discussions about the origin of john boats are like oldtimers explaining the difference between a whippoorwill and a whip-willow. (One sits with the limb. One sits across it. I can't recall which.) It is generally agreed john boats were first made from hand-hewn planks of hardwood, which means they were heavy when they had soaked up enough water to swell shut the cracks. They were built to carry loads in fast water, deep and shallow, which Ozark streams tend to be all the time except in flood. Today john boats are mostly aluminum, but they are still favored over canoes because they don't "tump" over as easily as canoes.

The bottom of a john boat is curved from back to front, and you soon learn how fast the river can spin a john boat crosswise in the current and fill it with water. So you listen when guides like Bland Wilson say, "Just put the back end where you want it to go. The river will take care of the front." Wilson could read the water better than any guide I ever knew. You stand in the back of a john boat to read the riffles. You want the boat to pass into the longest vee of quiet water in the shallows running over the rocky bottom. Most river guides will teach you how to run a boat if you keep quiet long enough. The entire point of floating a river is learning to be so quiet you can hear its voices.

* * * * *

Rivers and streams north of the Missouri River flow through rich farm land. The water runs murky to muddy, like the Missouri River. The current is often so slow that you don't float as much as you paddle. But the fishing can be good, and the creatures along the banks offer their own surprises. Most of the streams and rivers in Missouri have several public access points.

Rivers and streams south of the Missouri tend to be faster running, often spring fed and rocky bottomed. Those too small to float are wonderful streams to wade and fly fish for bluegill, sunfish, and bass. In the colder, spring-fed streams you can often catch rainbow trout.

Perhaps Missouri rivers and streams possess so much magic for me because I began learning their mysteries and adventures as a small boy wading and fly fishing the clear-water streams of central Missouri. But of all my river experiences, floating on the Missouri River has been the most inspiring. Once you overcome your fear of its size and power, the river carries you into another world. You begin to understand that part of America was discovered because men could not resist discovering the source of this mammoth flow.

Since our beginning, man has joined with the rivers for exploration and commerce. The flow of rivers is so strong we will always be called to gather there. I went to the rivers to fish as a boy. It would be many years before I understood the words of Thoreau: "Some men fish all their lives without knowing it is not really the fish they are after." I go to the rivers in time of joy and in times of sorrow. If I lived by an ocean, I would go there, but I live in Missouri where the rivers flow.

THE OZARKS

Some say the Ozarks is a magic place. The mystery and the beauty of places like the Irish Wilderness and Hercules Glades enchant many who wander deep into the forest.

The grandfathers and grandmothers of this country came to the Ozarks from Scotland and Ireland. These Scotch-Irish settlers traveled across the Smokies from Appalachia to land as rugged and beautiful as the hill country they left. The Ozark hills and valleys are well suited for the settlers' independent and secluded ways. Some say you can still hear the language of Shakespeare's time spoken in these hills.

The experience of walking in the Ozark wilderness reaches beyond the stories of what happens to those who find a different kind of energy here. The Ozark magic is not something the natives stand around the crossroads store

Limestone bluffs that once formed the shore of the Missouri River stand north of Jefferson City.

discussing. But every once in a while you see a knowing look in someone's eyes.

I know of no other way to tell you than to take you there, first on a walk alone into the Irish Wilderness, and then on a walk with others to the heart of Hercules Glades.

THE IRISH WILDERNESS

I had gone exploring in Missouri, this time on assignment to bring back some description of the place called the Irish Wilderness, part of Missouri's Mark Twain National Forest. As I traveled deeper into the Mark Twain, day to day concerns left me. The logging roads began calling out. Follow me, they seemed to say as an early spring breeze wooed through the pine. Follow me.

The Irish Wilderness covers parts of Carter, Ripley, Oregon, and Shannon Counties in southern Missouri. Highway 60 between Van Buren and Willow Springs runs along the northern boundary. The small town of Wilderness is near the center of this forest.

It was along the road to Wilderness that I passed a freshly closed grave. The red clay, ochre earth turned out of rocky soil, was covered with fresh-cut flowers and the tears of those who had buried their man that morning. My journey took me, somehow, to the widow's house. Her daughter listened as I stood on the porch asking directions to the trail into White's Creek cave above the Eleven Point River.

"We just buried her man," the daughter said to me. "The old woman is resting." I thanked her and was backing off the porch and quietly away from their time of grief when the old woman's voice came out of the back room: "Tell him," she said, and then she came out of the darkness to tell me herself. "Follow the path from the porch around the barn and down along the far corner of the hog pen. The trail you want begins there." She was old and dressed in sorrowing black. But her face had a light I have seen at the beginning of many journeys. Her eyes were clear. They had buried her man, but she would live on many years.

And so the journey began. I took only a topographical map, a compass, a camera, and the warning of hill people I had heard all my life: "Don't cross the ridge and you won't get lost."

I found the trail where the old woman said it was, and I began, calculating roughly a two hour walk to water. Maybe three more to the cave and back out again. Early on, a nail began eating through my sock. When I stopped for the first time I did not remove the boot. Instead I studied the map. I had followed the path, which ran in the bed of a dry creek. As I looked back, I saw I had reached the main creek bed, but there were three dry fingers joining to make the one where I now stood. Only one showed on the map. Which one had I followed? I knew this would be no ordinary journey.

After an hour, I still had found no water. The nail in my boot was working on the callous of my right heel. I stopped to consider the beauty around me. Holding the camera against my eye and propped on both elbows, I was able to focus on a wildflower momentarily. Looking up again without the camera, everything was moving in the shimmering aura of lush springtime in the deep forest.

I walked on, coming eventually to the spring. I plunged my face into the clean, cold water of the spring branch and drank my thirst away. I had walked five hours. I was not halfway to my destination. I took time to remove my boot, hammering the heel nail with two rocks. My sock was torn, the heel callous punctured and raw.

In the time it took to slow the nail's destruction, I made the decision to walk on toward the cave. It was the only way out, even though I might spend a chill, lonely night among the wilderness creatures. I knew there were still mountain lion in these hills and an occasional black bear. I was no longer concerned with the time of nightfall. The nail's damage dulled ordinary concerns within a few steps of my second beginning. The forest was still moving in its spring resonance. I walked on, full of the cold spring water, my hair still dripping from one last drink.

Man considers many things while walking alone in the forest for hours. Thirst, the pain of a nail gouging the right heel, the sound of invisible creatures rustling through the woods. Turtle or bear? The rustle of leaves in the silence of one man holding his breath is an intense experience. There were bear in these woods, but this was a turtle.

The trail steepened. I knew the climb would take me to White's Creek cave where I could begin my journey out of the forest. I was no longer lost in the woods. I was empty of thought, except for the pain in my heel, which touched my mind every other step. Between the pain, there was thirst. No other thoughts.

I reached the cave, pausing along the steep trail to look into darkness yawning at me from its entrance. The story a friend had told about a "black madonna" at the center of the cave's darkness lured me to the cave's mouth. But a primitive fear held me outside, as an animal stops at the edge of a

The statue of young Carver at the George Washington Carver National Monument near his boyhood home in Diamond commemorates this famous Missourian's later accomplishments.

cliff at night, sensing the absence of something. I could not enter.

I walked on, climbing the trail to the ridge overlooking the trees and the Eleven Point River. As I leaned against a black oak, the trees in the valley below were shimmering, an infinite progression of greens, as if light was a chorus of sound I could see and feel. Exhausted, I leaned against the tree, my mind as empty as the sky.

Suddenly my pulse raced with first sight of white and the bald eagle flying across my vision, inches beyond my reach. One. Two. Three bald eagles flying through my consciousness. I suppressed the urge of joy to holler as the three eagles, father, mother, and child, made their turn out over the valley of the river, circling back to land in a tree at the far end of the clearing less than seventy-five yards from where I stood.

The next period of time—minutes, hours, days—I stalked three eagles, wanting another look from just beyond arm's reach. Had they seen me? Would they allow another look closer to their roost? I thought of trees moving slowly toward each other in the breeze. I was calm, without thirst, or thought or pain, free in the moment of three eagles, the first I had ever seen.

I could see them watching me as I looked up from each careful step on fallen twigs and leaves of winter before spring. I reached a place within fifteen yards when the largest eagle made a small sound, lifting from the limb by the strong pull of his wings. Then the second eagle, more graceful than the first. And the third, with the start of a youngster left behind. I watched them soar out over the valley of the Eleven Point, my journey complete before it was finished.

Several times since I have seen the bald eagle, and more times than I can count I have watched the great blue heron flying just ahead of my journey along Missouri streams. Missouri is a place of endless possibilities. The trick is opening yourself to see.

HERCULES GLADES: TANEY COUNTY

Listen closely for the wilderness of voices. We are standing on a ridge in the middle of 12,000 acres called Hercules Glades. The sky is blue, cold, and clean. Only the wind speaks. Henry Rowe Schoolcraft, an early Ozark explorer, was one of the first to walk in this country and write what he saw:

"The country ... presented a character of unvaried sterility, consisting of a succession of lime-stone ridges, skirted with a feeble growth of oaks, with no depth of soil, often bare rocks upon the surface, and covered with coarse wild grass; and sometimes we crossed patches of ground of considerable extent without trees or brush of any kind, and resembling the Illinois prairies in appearance, but lacking their fertility and extent. Frequently these prairies occupied the tops of conical hills or extended ridges, while the intervening valleys were covered with oaks, giving the face of the country a very novel aspect, and resembling, when viewed in perspective, enormous sand-hills promiscuously piled up by the winds."

Schoolcraft, explorer and writer, spoke of what he saw one hundred and sixty years ago. The Glades are much the same today. The winds still blow across the ridges of the bald knobs called glades, carrying the history of the Hercules Glades Wilderness, a section of the Mark Twain National Forest deep in the Ozarks of Taney County, south of Springfield.

Early explorers took their bearings from the prominent elevations of Upper Pilot Knob, Lower Pilot Knob, and Coy Bald. From the ridge trail not far off the road to Hercules, the view of America reaches far into the distance. The promise beyond must have been great for many who stood here listening.

As the land eases back into a protected wilderness in the Mark Twain, there is winter timber, cedar, and blue sky. The greens of moss live deeper in the valleys as we walk toward the heart of Hercules Glades, a dry stream, barren except for the amazing color of its stone.

To know Missouri you must wander away from the beaten paths, taking smaller trails to quiet places where you may see creatures like the rainbow darter, the Western chorus frog, the Southern coal skink, the Acadian flycatcher, the cerulean warbler, the vesper sparrow, the meadow jumping mouse, and the sharp-shinned hawk. All of these can be found in Hercules Glades. Imagine a crisp, winter day walking where you have never been. Imagine the cerulean warbler. If you understand the value of such things, you can begin to appreciate the magnificent and subtle differences that are part of Missouri.

The dog keeps the same distance ahead on the trail, or off in the brush to the right or left of the trail, following his keen sense of smell: the scent of man; the scent of animals closer to his kind crossing the path he travels. There are five of us. And the dog, who will stop twice, telling me what animals

The old courthouse in St. Louis, built from 1831-1862, is architecturally unique in its blend of Greek revival and Italian renaissance architecture.

The Gateway Arch rises into the St. Louis sky, a magnificent structure of concrete and stainless steel that is a tribute to man's past and future explorations.

he has sensed. His mother was a coyote. He has run mostly among houses, but he remembers. The five are friends who spent the evening before in a house of native oak, talking and laughing with the fire in the stone fireplace.

The wind on the ridges keeps you moving in January. Temperature: 45 degrees.

The dog stops, sniffing the wind, then putting his nose back to the trail. He stops me with his look. I have walked a thousand walks with dogs in Missouri hills: with hounds who speak in wonderful tongues on the trail of rabbit, fox, raccoon, and deer; with this half-coyote dog I know so well he has become an extension of my consciousness in ways common to men and their dogs in these hills. He seems to say:

"Deer, crossing to the left." I walk to where he stopped and find fresh tracks of the doe. We walk on, dog in the lead again.

These twelve thousand three hundred and fifteen acres were declared the Hercules Glades Wilderness Area in 1976. Elevations in these Ozarks Highlands, sixty miles southwest of Springfield, range from seven hundred to thirteen hundred and forty feet near the Hercules lookout tower. The Hercules Glades Management Plan describes what you can find here:

"The glades have historically supported a tall grass prairie plant community which produces picturesque openings in the surrounding oak-hickory forest. Big blue stem, little blue stem, Indian grass, switch grass, prairie dropseed, and side oats gama are typical grasses associated with prairie forbs such as blackeyed Susan, cone flower, goldenrod, and various prairie clovers.

"South facing slopes are almost desert and are inhabited by such animal species as the collared lizard (mountain boomer) and the roadrunner more commonly at home in the arid southwest. The fringe tree, smoke tree, blue ash, and supplejack are characteristic woody plants found on the glades, but uncommon in the rest of the Ozark region. These plants, along with their associated insects, rodents, reptiles, amphibians, birds and mammals, go together to make the glade an unusual attraction in the Ozarks."

When I think of Missouri, the word I most want to use is diversity. Hercules Glades, deep in the Missouri Ozarks, is one of many places where you can find diversity. The forest management book lists twenty-nine species of fish, seventeen amphibians, thirty-four reptiles, ninety-two species of

birds, and thirty-nine different mammals found in Hercules Glades.

A botanist can find rare, threatened and endangered plants in the glades growing back toward its original wilderness: ciliate blue star, blazing star, stonecrop, Trelease's larkspur. I do not know the plants, but the names make me want to know.

The wind is rising from the valleys, lifting the hawks higher and higher. The mountain lion, the eastern timber wolf, and their prey, the bison and the elk, are gone. Smaller creatures remain. The dog stays out in front on the trail as we cross the last ridge and enter the final gradual descent to the valley of Long Creek.

After three hours of easy walking, the trail turns and drops into the bed of Long Creek and the magic begins. Here in the heart of Hercules Glades the creek is dry. In the lee of a rock ledge in the creek bed where rains race wild in the spring, there is quiet. The wind is only a breeze in the last valley. The few birds we have seen are silent in mid-afternoon feeding.

I rest against one of these rock shelves. The stone is blue, bed-rock blue, the same color as the winter sky. Nothing moves. As I lean into this slab of rock that hears water rolling the stones when the creek runs full, I hear more than I could hear before. I feel the stream moving in the stone, hear water rushing to become a river, feel the earth turning in this deep quiet.

The dog noses around the creek bed, finding a place in the bank grass on a south-facing slope where he curls and sleeps in one exhalation. We eat the dried fruit and nuts, the peanut butter and jelly sandwiches we have brought. We pass the canteen and drink the water as we sit in the hollow of large rocks out of the wind. The sun is warm. First one, then another, finds a south curl of grass, stretches out and follows the dog into short sleep. Only one goes on down the creek with his camera.

We wake in the order of our lying down. First the dog, then the rest of us. A few words, a holler down the creek to summon the fifth one. Then we start out of the valley of Long Creek, the warmth and the silence running full in our souls.

The short sleep, maybe twenty minutes, has been a meditation in a long walk of meditations. We have walked several hours. The climb up the trail makes breathing deeper. The air comes sharper, cleaner. At the top, the sky is blue, reaching beyond the far ridges. All parts of the universe seem in close harmony.

Winter in the Ozarks is a time of special beauty, when the forest stands dormant and blanketed in snow.

THE PEOPLE

"They were pure and clean and noble because they had just come from the stars — from among the stars, say the holy men. They were all Sky People, but when they descended to earth, the Sacred One, they found her divided into land and water, over which the Great Mysteries chose to send the wind howling like wolves, and to send down balls of ice to pound their heads, and breathe snow across the land, and cover the Sacred One with it, and to send screaming winds to steal the song-prayers from the Children's lips and clutch at the bodies beneath the buffalo robes with long, icy fingers. The Great Mysteries dropped funnel-shaped clouds from the sky and sent them dancing over the land, carrying away man and his pitiful little things into oblivion. Waters fell from the sky and the foaming water of the river swirled and sucked and roared, carrying dead buffalo on its back, and making the riverside walnuts and elm shake in fear. Surely at this time they must have made their first songs of death and mourning and supplication, cowering in their caves...

"But they came from the sky, say the Little Old Men; from among and of the stars. They were children up there as well, of Grandfather Sun, and as they say, noble and clean and shy and befuddled and inquisitive, just as might be expected, and immediately they began to explore."

The words of John Joseph Mathews writing in *The Osages: Children of the Middle Waters* tell us the Indians believed they came from the stars. The stories and rituals of the Osage are filled with their attempt to establish an order among themselves that matched the order they saw in the night sky.

The story of prehistoric man in Missouri remains a mystery. Some believe the Indians came from an ancient and distinct race of people, later displaced and perhaps exterminated by the Indians of historic times. No one sat on a distant hill recording the development of one civilization out of another. But a recent book, *American Genesis*, by Jeffrey Goodman, makes strong argument for the origin of man here. "Fully developed man has been in the Americas for at least 50,000 years," Goodman writes, "and possibly for as long as 250,000 years — far earlier than Homo Sapiens has been placed in the Middle East or anywhere else ... The American Indians are the patriarchs of the family tree."

Missouri was the meeting ground for the two greatest families of Indian tribes in North America, the Algonquin

and the Sioux. The Osage, Missouri, Kansas, Iowa, and Arkansas tribes were part of the Sioux nation. The Fox were among the many Algonquin tribes. When the warriors of the Fox encountered the warriors of the Missouri tribe, Missouri was named.

The Fox returned to their fires talking of the "mesisi-piya", or Mississippi, which in Fox meant "Big River." The Fox warriors spoke also of the "Big Canoe People" who lived at the confluence of the Missouri with the Mississippi River. The Fox word for "Big Canoe People" was "Missouri." The Missouris escaped the Fox warriors paddling up the river in their big canoes. The Missouris called themselves "Niutachi," "People Who Dwell at the Mouth of the River." Their Sioux word for the Missouri River was "Nishodse," which means "muddy water."

The Missouri and the Osage were the two main tribes inhabiting what is now called Missouri when the first European explorers came here, about the time written history of this state begins. The Osage, the "Wah-Sha-She" knew the "Ni-Sho-Dse" as the "Smoky Water People," their relatives in the Sioux nation. They also knew them as an occasional enemy when they paddled up the Missouri River to the Osage, and on up to the place where the Marais des Cygnes, the Little Osage, and the Marmiton rivers flow together. The Osage called this area of their villages the "Place of Many Swans," a marshy area near what is now the Schell-Osage Wildlife Area in Vernon County, northeast of Nevada.

As we look back in time, there is much speculation even among scholars trying to put together the earliest parts of man's story. We know the seas receded from the Ozarks about 500 million years ago. And the last glacier which covered the northern half of Missouri can be dated at 50,000 years ago. So it is possible that man as we know him could have evolved and begun his journeys in the southern half of Missouri, below the last glacier drained off by the Missouri River.

Among the books I have found, *The Osages: Children of the Middle Waters* tells the most interesting stories. Duane Meyer's *The Heritage of Missouri* is the best history. The story of the Osage Indians completes itself in their own words by Francis LaFlesche in *The Osage: Rite of the Chiefs, Sayings of the Ancient Men.*

The Osage were considered noble among the many tribes of North American Indians. As LaFlesche writes: "The Osage men were of impressive height, averaging six feet tall or more. Audubon considered them as 'well formed, athle-

Prevailing southwest winds on Stockton Lake in Cedar County provide fine sailing for the enthusiast.

tic and robust men of noble aspect.' The feats performed by their runners were remarkable, and indeed, it was not uncommon for the Osage to walk 60 miles in a day...

"The Osage subsisted chiefly through hunting, but they annually raised small crops of corn, beans, and pumpkins. The men hunted from May until August, returning in time to gather the crops left unhoed and unfenced during the summer. Late in September, the fall hunts began; these continued until about Christmas. The Indians then remained in their villages until February or March when the spring hunts commenced, first the bear, then the beaver hunt...

"Conspicuous among the various Indian tribes for their general sobriety, the Osage remained for more than a century but little changed by their association with white traders and visitors. 'You are surrounded by slaves,' old Chief Big Soldier once remarked to a white friend. 'Everything about you is in chains, and you are in chains yourselves. I fear if I should change my pursuit for yours, I, too, should become a slave.'"

Everything I have read about the Indians who lived in Missouri suggests they lived a simpler life than ours, but their lives were also filled with mystery and frustrations while they sought an order among themselves as complete and peaceful as the order of stars they saw in the night sky.

* * * * *

Missouri is a meeting place of tribes. In the beginning, the tribes were herds of buffalo. Eventually, the Indian tribes mingled their footprints with the hoofprints of the wandering herds. When they paused in their travels to gather around the fires, they told stories. And in the stories of the wise ones among the Osage, who were called "The Little Old Men," we hear the names they spoke, and we can imagine something of their ways:

"Star That Came to Earth" comes from stories of their beginning; "Bald Eagle People" speaks of noble people among them; "They Who Make Clear the Way" were their leaders in journeys of body and spirit; "Travelers in the Mist" were those among the tribes who traveled along the rivers; "The Awakeners" were those, like the sun, who spoke of new days, new things; "Night People" and "Cedar Star" speak of Osage beliefs in the stars of night; "Men of Mystery" were those among them who knew of other ways, other lives.

The Osage did not consider themselves the center of the universe. They were only part of The Sacred One as the winds are part of the sky and the hawk soaring there. The Osage believed the rushing waters of the stream were the means of reaching old age. They called the willow "the tree that never dies." They believed they came from the stars.

Whatever their origin, the Indians are part of our story. Their ways have mingled with ours: tribe flowing into tribe; Indian nation flowing into the nation of those who came to America from Europe. Missouri's location is an essential part of this story. The Mississippi River has always been a great dividing line in America. And the Missouri River has always been a great avenue of discovery and commerce.

The story of Missouri's settlement by the Europeans is a story that follows the earliest explorers along the Mississippi River: the Spanish coming up river from the south and the French coming down river from the north. We know the earliest journeys of explorers followed the rivers just as the Iowas paddled their canoes up the Des Moines, just as the Arkansas, the Osage, and the Missouris paddled up the rivers that now carry their Indian names.

When the white man came, he followed the Indians up the same rivers seeking furs that opened American commerce. When the next migration of Europeans came, the settlers, they traveled the same rivers. The story I tell here can catch only a glimpse of the Indians before the white settlers came.

If you study the maps of Missouri in a chronological order, you can see America reaching out along its rivers discovering itself. A map showing "Population Origins in Rural Missouri" places the German immigrants along the Missouri River. They took rich bottom land for farms, although they did not find the land ready for planting. North of the Missouri River most of the immigrants came from Kentucky-Virginia, Kentucky-Ohio, and Indiana-Ohio-Illinois. The routes of migration through southern Missouri are marked Kentucky-Tennessee and Tennessee-Kentucky showing the continuation that began when the Scotch-Irish left Appalachia for the hill country of the Ozarks.

The diversity of people living in Missouri can be found in the smaller settlements shown on this map, including a significant number of black settlements in early rural Missouri. Immigrants to Missouri in the last half of the nineteenth century included Austrian, Belgian, Bohemian, Czechoslovakian, Danish, Dutch, French, Greek, Hungarian, Irish, Italian, Polish, Russian, Swiss, Swedish, Welsh, Yugoslovian, Amish, and Mennonite. When you add this rural mixture to the ethnic neighborhoods in St. Louis and

The austere interior of Flintlock Church, reconstructed in Old Missouri Town, dates from 1840.

Kansas City, Missouri becomes an interesting blend of cultures, traditions, and people.

* * * * *

SMALL TOWNS

The settlement of Missouri's farms and small towns was repeated over and over in towns like Westphalia in central Missouri. Much of Missouri began as Westphalia began. I want to tell you the story of this small town because it reaches across the years from our first settlemenets to a way of life some say is ending. You find the values of a people when you look into the lives of quieter places. Cities hold the vision of our future, but small towns open into a way of life still sought by many. The story of Westphalia reaches across time from the Indian villages to our big cities. Much of what lies between then and now can still be found in the small towns of Missouri.

WESTPHALIA

Westphalia is a quiet place where the flow of time has carved beauty out of a valley that holds the final, sweeping bends of the Maries River. They called it Maria Creek when the first German families settled here in 1835. Before that the ridge that now holds the majestic stone church looked down into a large Indian village.

And before that, prehistoric tribes took strength from the rich earth and buried their dead on a mound overlooking the confluence of the Maries and Osage rivers just beyond this town. The quiet held men gathered around the flickering camp fire at the mouth of the river. They spoke the myths of men before them. As the call of wild animals reached their night circle, they spoke of the white man who was coming.

By June 1804, when the men of the Lewis and Clark expedition camped at the mouth of the Osage where it joins the Missouri, the Osage Indians were gone. Lewis and Clark would go all the way to the Pacific Ocean, returning to St. Louis in 1806 with a map opening the way west.

Thirty-two years later Ferdinand Helias, a Belgian nobleman and a Jesuit missionary who had come to America to work with the Indians, set out by steamboat up river from St. Louis. Among his traveling companions were Father Pierre DeSmet, on his way to being the "Apostle of the Indians," and John Sutter, on his way to discover gold in California.

Father Helias, then forty-two, grew impatient when the

The Arrow Rock Bank stands abandoned, a symbol of 19th-century commerce and prosperity along the Missouri River.

steamboat broke down on May 11. Leaving the boat, he rode on horseback along the north bank of the Missouri, in what is now Callaway County, to the village of Côte Sans Dessein. Perhaps he was looking for someone who could show him the river crossing to the small group of German Catholic immigrants who had sent for a priest. The next day he reached their settlement where the Maries flows into the Osage at a place then called Lisletown.

But something about the place did not suit him. Perhaps he disliked the whiskey and swearing of the fur traders. Or maybe the spring-fed Maria Creek called to him. For whatever reasons, Father Helias moved on.

Chances are good the priest rode along the Indian trail from burial mound to village until he found the valley. Nicholas Hesse was among the German immigrants already settled there. He had been farming along the "beautiful stream . . . of many fish" since 1835.

"It has fertile bottomland, level valleys, and nearly everywhere rich land on the surrounding hills," Hesse wrote. "The region is excellently suited for cattle-raising, and will probably be populated mainly by industrious Germans, who seem to have concentrated there for some years and appear to displace the American, who is fond of wandering."

And so it would be. Father Helias rode the ridge to where the church now stands and decided this would be the center of New Westphalia.

But not without more hard work than some could bear. Hesse was among those who would not stay. In 1838, after returning to Germany, he wrote *Western North America* for those who might seek their dreams in places like this. To offset earlier, glowing accounts of pioneer life, Hesse urged a realistic approach to the new world.

"Whoever is well situated in Europe, or even somewhat satisfactorily so, should not move . . . Corn soup, corn bread, and fried bacon — if incidentally they owned some — had in the beginning to be substituted for the much-lauded game roasts."

Quoting an old proverb, Hesse wrote: "All beginning is difficult." Hesse told would-be pioneers what he had seen coming up the river to New Westphalia. The river bottom land was overgrown "with a dense, often impenetrable forest." He saw sycamores and cottonwoods . . . often thirty feet in circumference. The white oak often has a diameter of 6 or 7 feet and a height up to 50 feet without branches.

"The richness of the soil — producing corn stalks of

twenty feet in height — is without comparison." But "the region from Gasconade to Maria Creek is rough and not suitable for farming." Nonetheless Hesse found and purchased land. "The farm which I bought on Maria Creek had twenty-five acres of cultivated land with the necessary loghouses for dwellings and stables," he wrote.

"It sounds agreeable indeed to the ear of a German when one speaks of the purchase of an acre of land at $2.50, but if the cost of clearing and cultivating of the land and the erection of the buildings are taken into consideration, then the cost per acre is at least $10, and for that one can buy anywhere in Missouri cultivated farms with about twenty to thirty acres ready for crop."

Hesse recorded that a horse cost $50, a cow with calf $15, a wagon $60, a sled $2, a saddle with two bridles $12, and three dozen chickens $5. "One hundred pounds of fresh pork cost $3 in the fall of 1853. However, a year later $4.50 to $5 was paid in the regions around the Missouri and Osage."

More people came, some with the $1,000 Hesse said they would need to get a start in Missouri, some without. Hesse described the mental journey the German immigrants might expect. First "they have yet the brightly colored ideas ... from travel accounts and letters ..." Then "it begins to dawn on many that the lesson they have learned is indeed a bitter one ... False shame still prevents them from being quite honest with themselves. When this feeling of shame is overcome, then ... many discover that the happiness of mankind cannot be reached by a flight into the woods, but depends on something quite different. The gist of the whole matter is contained in the simple saying: 'Search for happiness not outside but within yourself, and be satisfied with the station in which Providence has placed you! To be satisfied and to satisfy others is the highest happiness on earth.'"

But the urge for a new life in America was strong, and the settlers kept coming, fueled by dreams of a better life.

Father Helias and his parishioners built a simple log church. By the end of his first year there, more than one hundred families lived in New Westphalia. By 1840, there were six hundred people in and around the settlement. Helias lived in the log church, probably sleeping on the floor of the loft above the sacristy. On the sacristy door, he attached this verse: "Those who aspire to hard work, who needs to go among the red-skinned Indians? It is sufficient

to live at Westphalia; there everything is rough work." And so it was in the beginning of the settlement of Missouri.

* * * * *

Today Westphalia has a quiet strength as solid as the stone church built in 1848. We are a long way beyond our ancestors but the rich river valley and the beauty of the spring-fed stream flowing into big rivers were surely part of their decision to stay.

Joe Redel is one of those who spent most of his life in this place. During his last years he lived in one room of his ten-room house on the main street just east of the church. His view of Westphalia spanned ninety-three years. I talked with him not long before he died.

"I was born and raised here. At my age, I can't recall everything. I don't make no garden no more. I don't make nothin' no more."

But he enjoyed talking. He left the farm for St. Louis where he worked in the First National Bank from 1913 to 1923. But the city and the responsibilities of balancing the bank's general account wore on him until he wanted no more of it. So he came back to a simpler life on the farm. "I came back to Westphalia because I was gettin' nervous. That's the best thing anybody can do. Man is his own boss. Yeah, this is the best place.

"They ain't much going on. Settled here mostly by Germans. Old Germans, you know, settled everywhere. Some of 'em done good. Some of 'em didn't. Some went back to Germany. And those people that settled along the rivers, they had to have good land. And they could make it. Others settled on the hillside. They didn't make it and left. We had a time here when we had only one family that couldn't speak German. And that was the doctor ... But that was the only family. And the kids all were raised in the Catholic School. But they're all gone."

Westphalia is still mostly German. All but a few families attend St. Joseph's Catholic Church.

As we talk, one of his daughters comes by to check on her father. She opens the south window for more breeze, exchanges a few words, brings in his St. Louis Globe-Democrat, then goes her way. In a short while, the second daughter stops by with her husband. They have retired from St. Louis to an 89-acre farm on the east hills overlooking Westphalia.

Talk centers on city life: asphalt parking lots, noise, money. "You can't get no privacy," the old man says. "You

Wilson's Creek National Battlefield south of Springfield, commemorates the site of Missouri's best known Civil War battle.

can't get nowhere walking." The two St. Louis papers he reads every day, the Globe and the Post-Dispatch, tell him about the fuel shortage. "These little country towns are buildin' up, buildin' up real fast," the son-in-law puts in. "People movin' out," the old man says. Coming back to "good churches, good schools." The 1980 census shows the increased popularity of small towns in Missouri.

I leave them talking as the breeze blows in the cool room where Joe Redel spends his hours.

Beyond the church in the other direction, another man of years works in his garden. He is known and loved by everyone who knows this town. Joe Luebbert owned the tavern from 1931 until he retired after forty years. Now he gardens, fishes, and visits with those who come to talk in the living room of the house he built just before he sold the tavern where he had lived above the business.

Joe Luebbert's was far more than a tavern. It was the gathering place of young and old, and it came to have the personality of the man who owned it and worked behind the bar from 7:30 every morning until 11 o'clock at night, seven days a week. I never heard anyone call it anything but "Joe Luebbert's" in all my years of going there. I can still hear the ticking of the clock that hung on the wall. Joe Luebbert's is no more. But once, in the evenings, the old-timers gathered at their table near the front for pinochle, speaking in German, the only language for the game as they learned to play it.

The tavern sat on the corner of the main street across from the front doors of the church. "You know what the people liked the most?" Joe asked in his German accent. "On Sundays, when you come out of church, you come in there — or during the week time. The old people come to town. Their wives would go to the store and do some shopping, and the old people come in here and get himself a half-pint, maybe three or four men together. And each one take his part out of that, and then they go home when their wives were done shopping. That's all they would drink. You go to Mass first . . .

"But what a difference now. Used to (be a) bottle of sodie when I started was 5 cents. Now 35. Seven times as high. Money ain't worth nothin' no more."

When Joe married, he left the family farm and bought the tavern. The first three years before electricity and refrigeration, he cut ice off the creek every winter and stored it in the ice house behind the tavern to keep his beer cold in the summer. "I started just a year before whiskey and beer came back." During that last year of prohibition, he sold only "near beer, one-half of one percent" alcohol.

Joe had married the daughter of Judge Ben Schauwecker, a banker who was sentenced to a year in prison for selling liquor from his home. When he got out of prison in 1931, Schauwecker told a Kansas City Star reporter he had enjoyed his stay in federal prison.

"Worry? What about? I hadn't done any wrong. I had a clear conscience. I sold wine and beer and whiskey, yes, but that's not wrong. We don't respect that prohibition law." When Schauwecker went off to prison, the account said, three hundred of the five hundred townspeople escorted him to the train in Jefferson City, the state capital, fourteen miles away.

"Our forefathers in Prussia made and drank their beer and wine and schnapps for a thousand years without harm to themselves or anyone else. It's been ninety-six years since our people came from Westphalia (a province in Germany) and settled here, and after they had built log cabins to live in the next thing they did was to build a church and a brewery."

Prohibition closed the brewery. But as Schauwecker told the reporter, "If there is a home without its wine or beer or whiskey, I don't know it."

Westphalia, Joe Luebbert will tell you, has always been a good beer drinking town. And a religious town, as you can see for yourself any Sunday. Some say a simple reverence for the Lord's beauty makes the town what it is. "I don't know," Joe Luebbert said when asked why he thought the town was such a special place. "They keep it nice and clean all over. And people are awful friendly, I think.

"It's an awful solid place . . . They work together real good. If somebody has trouble, you can just step out the door and holler. I don't care if it's your enemy or your friend, he comes and helps . . . They stick together.

"I'm gonna stay here 'til I die, by God. This is the place."

* * * * *

Wheat dries in shocks along the road to Westphalia. In the next field, modern machines are turning hay into giant round bales. Everywhere you find the contrasts of the old world and the new; in the eyes of the old men, in the voices of the young boys kicking their soccer ball against the stone wall that borders school yard and church. You can hear the faint accents of Germany six and seven generations beyond Nicholas Hesse and the first immigrants to Westphalia.

Stone lily pads, formed by thousands of years of seeping water, lie deep inside Onondaga Cave at Onondaga Cave State Park.

The church bell tolls the late afternoon hour. The day is hot. The sky is blue. The streets are quiet. Cattle move up from the cool shade of the Maries to graze in the pastures of evening light. The peacefulness is as clean and simple as the breeze that nudges the old man in his last years in this town with the quiet name Westphalia.

THE CITIES

The spirit of a people can be found in the quieter places, but the vision of a people and the reach of their dreams can be found in cities like St. Louis and Kansas City. Like the rivers that come together in both cities, St. Louis and Kansas City are gathering places in the heart of America. Both cities are part of Missouri, and yet both are as different from the rest of Missouri as they are from each other. St. Louis looks east, Kansas City looks west. St. Louis has a history and a future based in industry. Kansas City is the center of America's emerging agricultural nation. Perhaps they can best be understood as inland ports served by barge lines, railroads, trucklines and airlines.

St. Louis was founded in 1764 as a fur trading post at the confluence of the Missouri and the Mississippi rivers. Pierre Liguest Laclede was a "well born, well educated Frenchman who had come to New Orleans in 1755." The fur trade lured him up river. Laclede placed his 13-year old stepson, Auguste Chouteau, in charge of 30 men who began construction of the fur trading post that was the beginning of St. Louis.

Chouteau's journal quotes Laclede: "I have found a site on which to form my settlement which might hereafter become one of the finest cities of America." The fur trappers brought in their furs, and the settlement on the west bank of the Mississippi River grew.

Barely thirty-nine years had passed when St. Louis became the center of a new America. In 1803, the United States purchased the Louisiana Territory, 828,000 square miles, for about $15,000,000. The treaty, dated September 30, 1803, and signed several days later, doubled the domain of the United States. President Thomas Jefferson chose St. Louis as the site of the formal takeover of the territory from the French under the reign of Napoleon Bonaparte.

On May 14, 1804, the Lewis and Clark Expedition left the mouth of the Missouri River on a journey of exploration that opened America to the Pacific Ocean. At noon on September 23, 1806, two years, four months, two days and 7,000

miles later, the expedition returned to St. Louis. The west was open with a mapped route to the Pacific, and America was on its way to becoming one of the greatest nations of the world.

The story of Missouri in modern history begins with the journey of Lewis and Clark. Less than 200 years have passed since their expedition in 1804. By 1812, Missouri was organized as a territory, and entered the union of the United States in 1821.

As Missouri grew along the rivers, St. Louis grew. The Old Courthouse was begun in 1839 and finished in 1862. Henry Clay, Stephen Douglas, and Thomas Hart Benton, the Senator, would argue their cases here. But the courthouse was made famous by a slave named Dred Scott who sued for his freedom in 1846. Although Scott won his claim to freedom in the lower court, the Missouri Supreme Court overturned the decision. Eventually that decision by the state appellate court was upheld by the U.S. Supreme Court, but the stage was now set for the question of slavery to be decided in the Civil War.

Ulysses S. Grant, who had been forced to resign from the army because of his drinking, came to St. Louis as a struggling Illinois farmer to sell cord wood at Soulard Market. Grant also married a St. Louis girl. Another Civil War General, William Tecumseh Sherman, was stationed in St. Louis for a time before the Civil War. And Abraham Lincoln practiced law in Springfield, Illinois, about 125 miles from St. Louis.

Missouri was squarely in the middle of the Civil War with parts of the state pro-slavery and parts for the abolition of slavery. Through all of it, St. Louis grew from a fur trading post into an industrial city.

The Eads Bridge spanning the Mississippi River in 1874 joined St. Louis to the railroads of the east. Perhaps the people of the time understood what that would mean to their city because they held a parade said to be 14 miles long in honor of the bridge opening.

In 1891, Elias Wainwright, a wealthy St. Louis businessman, commissioned the design of the Wainwright Building by Louis Henry Sullivan. The Wainwright Building became one of America's first skyscrapers, standing at the beginning of its architectural era.

Washington University, today one of the country's leading private universities, was founded as the first nonsectarian college in the middle west in 1853 by William Greenleaf Eliot, a Unitarian minister and grandfather of

The Burfordville covered bridge, 140-feet long, spans the Whitewater River in Cape Girardeau County.

poet T. S. Eliot. St. Louis University has been operated by the Jesuits since 1827, and towns like Westphalia often have a Jesuit missionary in their history.

Forest Park, named for its 1,374 acres of forest, was made part of the city in 1874. Later other signs of affluence appeared. Henry Shaw, who came to St. Louis from Sheffield, England, as a young man of 19, retired a wealthy man 20 years later. Shaw's first gift to St. Louis was the Missouri Botanical Garden. Later he gave the city 285 acres for Tower Grove Park.

Part of the story of St. Louis only can be found in its wonderful neighborhood taverns, and in the many ethnic neighborhoods that still reflect the charm and hold to the customs of the old world. When you walk the streets of the Italian neighborhood called The Hill, you begin to feel the reach of St. Louis in its people, people who have come to St. Louis from many places in the world. St. Louis has a wonderful abundance of good food and music from river town blues to progressive jazz. But you learn St. Louis best in its neighborhoods, Irish, Italian, Black, German, and others.

There is no better place to sample the old world flavor of St. Louis than at Soulard Market. In 1842, Madame Julie Soulard, widow of Antoine Soulard, surveyor general of the Upper Louisiana Territory under Spanish rule, donated land to be used for the market. On Saturday mornings one hundred forty years later, St. Louis still gathers at the Soulard.

The history of St. Louis can be told in many ways, in many pages. The spirit of the place is less easy to capture. You must go to Soulard. Go to Forest Park. Tour the Anheuser-Busch brewery. Smell the orchids of Shaw's garden. Walk the sidewalks of the fashionable Central West End, where ladies and gentlemen of this century gather at sidewalk cafes.

If I could take you to only one place in St. Louis, I would take you on a full moon night to stand under the Gateway Arch. St. Louis stands at the confluence of America's two greatest rivers, the Missouri and the Mississippi, and this magnificent arch rising 630 feet into the sky is the symbol of what St. Louis has become. The arch stands as a tribute to the Lewis and Clark Expedition opening the west, but it arches into the sky from the spirit and the vision of the people of St. Louis.

The Gateway Arch reaches into the future. This beautiful structure of concrete and stainless steel stands as the result of one man's vision. That man, Eero Saarinen, was an archi-

tect who came from Finland with his father, Eeliel Saarinen, also an architect. The dream of this arch began when Eero Saarinen was a young man and was completed after he died.

Eeliel Saarinen once said to his son: "Always think of the next larger thing." The next larger thing in the history of St. Louis always has been the future. From Pierre Laclede's fur trading cabin, through the Lewis and Clark Expedition, to the solo, transatlantic flight of Charles Lindbergh in *The Spirit of St. Louis*, to the Mercury and Gemini space capsules built by the McDonnell Douglas Corporation, the vision of St. Louis reaches into all areas of the future from its history as a great city.

Today St. Louis is a city of 2,500,000 people living in the metropolitan area. The City of St. Louis, which has not changed its boundaries since 1876, has a population of 454,000. But St. Louis reaches out in a vast metropolitan sprawl of smaller municipalities like Clayton, University City, Kirkwood, Webster Groves, Florissant, and a long list of many others. The St. Louis metropolitan area fans out to fill the huge valley where the Missouri and Mississippi flow together. St. Louis faces east, and much of the city, from its age to its wealth, is more like an eastern city than any of the rest of Missouri.

Kansas City rises up from the prairie and seems to face toward the west. The metropolitan area of Kansas City reaches in all directions with a population of 1,500,000. The city of Kansas City has a population of 448,000, ranking 27th behind St. Louis, 26th in the nation. The combined populations of these two metropolitan areas total 4,000,000. The total population of Missouri is approximately 5,000,000.

A closer look at the increases and decreases in population since the 1970 Census shows that the Kansas City metropolitan area is growing at a faster rate than the St. Louis area. A 10-year span is hardly long enough to predict a trend, but professional observers say Kansas City will become the larger of the two cities in the next century, and one of the most important cities in the world because of its location at the center of what one writer calls the emerging "Breadbasket Nation" of America.

Kansas City began at the confluence of the Kansas River, called the Kaw, and the Missouri River where it makes a bend from the north to flow east to St. Louis. When the first settlers came up river from St. Louis and reached this bend in the Missouri, they left their boats to travel overland.

The Watkins Mansion and nearby mill were built in Clay County in 1860 by Waltus L. Watkins, heralding industrial revolution in northern Missouri.

Kansas City had its beginning where the overland trails began.

Originally, there were two frontier settlements: the Town of Kansas on the Missouri River and Westport, four miles south of the river on the Sante Fe Trail. The Town of Kansas began as the Grand Village des Canzes, named for the Kansas Indians. Kansas means "South Wind People." The first explorers came to the confluence of the Missouri and the Kaw following rumors of silver. They did not find silver, but they took back boats loaded with furs.

François Chouteau, an employee of the American Fur Company, built a trading post in the Kaw River bottom in the spring of 1821. The riverboat *Independence* had proven the Missouri river navigable by steamboat in 1819, and the settlers began arriving by boat to begin their overland journeys from Chouteau's settlement. Jackson County was organized in 1826, with a county seat about 10 miles east at Independence, at the head of the Santa Fe Trail and the Oregon Trail.

In 1832 an enterprising merchant named John Calvin McCoy built a store along the trail in what is now Westport. McCoy platted Westport a year later. He wanted to get the business of the wagon trains returning from the southwest, and to catch some of the overflow business from Independence. Meanwhile Chouteau had established a new business at the ferry landing, called Westport Landing, on the Missouri River, four miles north of McCoy's Westport.

In 1838 a man named John Augustus Sutter came up river from St. Louis. McCoy outfitted Sutter for his travels to Santa Fe, and on to Sacramento where Sutter built a fort and established a settlement in California. In 1848, Sutter's partner in a sawmill venture, James W. Marshall, found gold at Sutter's Mill. The word raced back east and towns like Westport and young Kansas City flourished in the 1849 gold rush. According to one account, "within a period of five months during 1848-9, some 900 wagons started on their journey from the village. About 2,000 travelers were outfitted here in trade estimated at $5 million."

A cholera epidemic interrupted the boom times, but on February 22, 1853, a charter was obtained incorporating the village as "The City of Kansas." By 1855, most of the overland trade had returned, and Kansas City began to grow.

The Civil War took its toll on progress until 1864 when the last major battle in the west was fought at the Battle of Westport, called the "Gettysburg of the West." In 1865,

when the war had ended, the Missouri Pacific Railroad arrived in Kansas City from St. Louis.

In 1869, the Hannibal Bridge, the first crossing the Missouri River, was completed, connecting Kansas City with Chicago and establishing a link with world markets. In 1870 the first stockyards were built. Kansas City was becoming a trade center for cattle and grain. Russian Mennonite immigrants planted winter turkey red wheat in 1874. Today, the Kansas City Board of Trade is the world's largest marketplace for that winter wheat, and the Russians are buying it back by the shipload.

Kansas City, the city of the "South Wind People," was now on its way to becoming one of America's most beautiful cities. It is said there are more fountains in Kansas City than in any other city in the world. Kansas City's beautification began when a newspaper publisher named William Rockhill Nelson started *The Kansas City Star* in 1880. Nelson, using his newspaper, became a one-man crusade for city streets, parks, and boulevards. Today the William Rockhill Nelson Gallery of Art stands at the head of a magnificent lawn in tribute to the publisher.

Today Kansas City faces into its future. In a recent book, *The Nine Nations of North America*, author Joel Garreau calls Kansas City the capital of an emerging "Breadbasket Nation." Garreau's Breadbasket Nation includes a large part of Texas and Oklahoma, all of Kansas, eastern Colorado, about half of Missouri, the fertile half, part of Illinois, all of Iowa and Nebraska, part of Wisconsin, and all of Minnesota, South Dakota, and North Dakota, reaching into the agricultural regions of southern Canada.

"The Breadbasket," Garreau writes, "controls more of the world's wheat than the Arab world controls oil." Kansas City, which Garreau sees as the capital of this fertile new nation of food suppliers, "is strategically more important than Saudi Arabia." Food will become more important than oil.

Along the streets of Kansas City today there is a new spirit of opportunity and enterprise. Impressed by the beauty of Kansas City's parks, fountains, and tree-shaded boulevards, promoters are calling Kansas City "America's most livable city."

In the 1930s, Kansas City was known as a wide open town. Night clubs flourished and jazz musicians came to Kansas City to play. Today jazz is still part of Kansas City's heritage, and the International Women's Jazz Festival is held here. Cultural trends come and go, but two of Kansas

The Harry S. Truman birthplace in Lamar is typical of the small but elegant residences found in western Missouri in the 1880's.

City's landmarks suggest what has been and what the city will become.

In the 1920s, a developer named J.C. Nichols built the Country Club Plaza, America's first shopping center and today a masterpiece of beauty and planning. Nichols also developed the surrounding neighborhoods, establishing home associations to maintain a standard of beauty in Kansas City's suburban development. The Country Club Plaza area remains a landmark of excellence for all cities.

Another entrepreneur, Joyce Hall, came to Kansas City selling penny postcards. He built Hallmark Cards as the center of his enterprise. In 1964, Hall asked his employees what they would want in a complex where they could both live and work. Today Crown Center, the realization of that dream, is called a "city of the future within a city." The Crown Center complex containing hotels, expensive condominiums, shops, restaurants, and office buildings is another indication of Kansas City's vision of the future.

The spirit of Kansas City is young and optimistic, as if the people here know their city, already a beautiful place to live, is also becoming a leader in world markets. Kansas Citians are proud of the 1,346-acre Swope Park and the Harry S. Truman Sports Complex. Kansas City has recently completed restoration and expansion of the Truman Medical Center. The Nelson Gallery and the Kansas City Art Institute, founded in 1921, stand as proof of the city's dedication to the arts.

The true spirit of Kansas City can be found along its streets and boulevards. From jazz to barbecue, from Westport, now a restored area of restaurants and shops, to Crown Center, Kansas City's dream reaches into a promising future.

*   *   *   *   *

What is the promise of this place called Missouri and the people who live here? Surely the weather plays a part, as it always has, in our resilience. And Missouri's location. From the beginning of our civilization, Missouri has been a place of beginnings in commerce and exploration.

We mine the rich Viburnum Trend. Geologists believe Missouri sits atop some of the richest mineral deposits in the world. We grow some of the world's finest burley, a light brown tobacco that hangs to dry each year in the barns of northwest Missouri around Weston. We don't pick cotton by hand anymore, but we grow it and bale it in the Bootheel of southeastern Missouri. We produce the world's largest

supply of white oak for whiskey barrels, and some fine moonshine. Missouri's production ranges from aerospace technology to the fashioning of john boat paddles out of sassafras.

Missouri has preserved almost three million acres of its 68,995 square miles in federal and state wildlife and recreation areas. There are 400,000 acres of lake water, and 11,000 miles of permanently flowing rivers and streams.

Missouri's highway system is considered one of the best in the world. West of St. Louis, along one of Missouri's most beautiful roads, Highway 94, that follows the north bank of the Missouri River to Jefferson City, Missouri wines are aging, gaining a reputation that one day may rival the great French wines. Like its weather, Missouri's diversity of place, products, and people are its treasures.

Those who claim to know say the nation's next crisis will be the fight over water for dry areas of the United States where population is booming. As I write, proposals are being discussed to divert excess water from the Missouri River into eastern Colorado, or lower down river, from St. Joseph, Missouri, to Dodge City, Kansas, through irrigation canals.

Since the 1940s, 16 million acres of land in the high plains states of Texas, New Mexico, Oklahoma, Colorado, Kansas, and Nebraska have come under irrigation. There are those who believe the water shortage is so serious that the Ogallala Aquifer, the underground reservoir that has been tapped to water this growth of farming, will be pumped dry between the year 2000 and 2020.

Time will tell whether water becomes an issue great enough to cause another civil war. But, for now, Missouri rides at the center of the nation with enough water flowing in the Missouri and the Mississippi and our other rivers to irrigate our needs.

Other changes are developing in America, and Missouri sits squarely in the middle of the nation. As Garreau writes, "If you draw a line through the country from San Francisco to New York, the two commercial centers on either coast, everything has to come through Kansas City." And through Missouri. Once again Missouri will be on the frontier feeding a large part of the world. Once again the Missouri River and the Mississippi River will carry the commerce of the emerging Breadbasket Nation as these rivers have carried so much of our history and development.

The promise of Missouri is the promise of its people. Beginning with the noble Osage Indians, Missouri's heri-

Century-old maples trickle sap into syrup pails at Mill Stream Gardens, east of Fredericktown.

On April 3, 1860, the first Pony Express rider left these stables in St. Joseph, beginning the 2,000-mile trip to Sacramento.

tage of people is rich, famous, and infamous. The list includes Harry S. Truman, Frank and Jesse James; Emmett Kelly, the clown, and Walt Disney; George Washington Carver and Dr. Tom Dooley; the poet Langston Hughes and the musician Scott Joplin; J.C. Penney and Joyce Hall; George Caleb Bingham and Thomas Hart Benton. Missouri has nourished some wonderful dreams. Many of the people "raised up in Missouri" have given the wealth of those dreams to people all over the world.

The stories of their lives are part of the story that is Missouri. I finish this story with a few words from the poet, John Neihardt. He was my teacher and my friend, and much of what he wrote tells the story of Missouri in a grand way. Neihardt lived among the Indians as a young man. He wrote of an earlier time in America when the white man's civilization had begun to replace the lives of the Indians. What he wrote then has more to say today than he could have known. He wrote the stories of men like Black Elk, the last medicine man of the Ogallala Sioux, who passed his vision on to Neihardt.

The Indians called John Neihardt, "Flaming Rainbow." They could see the joy in his eyes, the beauty his life would become. In his twilight years, a time of clear blue eyes and flowing white hair, when most of his major work was done, Neihardt gathered around him those who would listen. He loved the young. Many of us listened as students at the University of Missouri. When we were quiet, the old man opened the book of his life and told the stories he had written there, rarely consulting the printed page. It was spring, a time he loved. We were young, and so was he. In his poem, "April Theology," he said:
"God and I dream the vast dreams together.
 We are one in the doing of things that are done and to be:
 I am part of my God as a raindrop is part of the sea!"
The unceasing journey of Missouri continues with the wind and the rivers.

Late winter light outlines trees along Paddy Creek, which flows into the Big Piney River in the Mark Twain National Forest south of Rolla.

Above: Mina Sauk Falls, the highest in Missouri, cascade 132 feet, a mile southwest of Taum Sauk Mountain in Iron County. The falls are named after Chief Taum Sauk's daughter. *Left:* The flowering dogwood, the state tree of Missouri, is a spring-flowering beauty usually found in rugged woods south of the Missouri River like these in Lake of the Ozarks State Park.

Above: Log cabins and walnut trees are reminders of settlers who found beautiful homesites like this one in the Huckleberry Ridge State Forest in McDonald County. *Right:* These rock carvings, called petroglyphs, are signs of some of Missouri's earliest inhabitants preserved in Washington State Park near Old Mines.

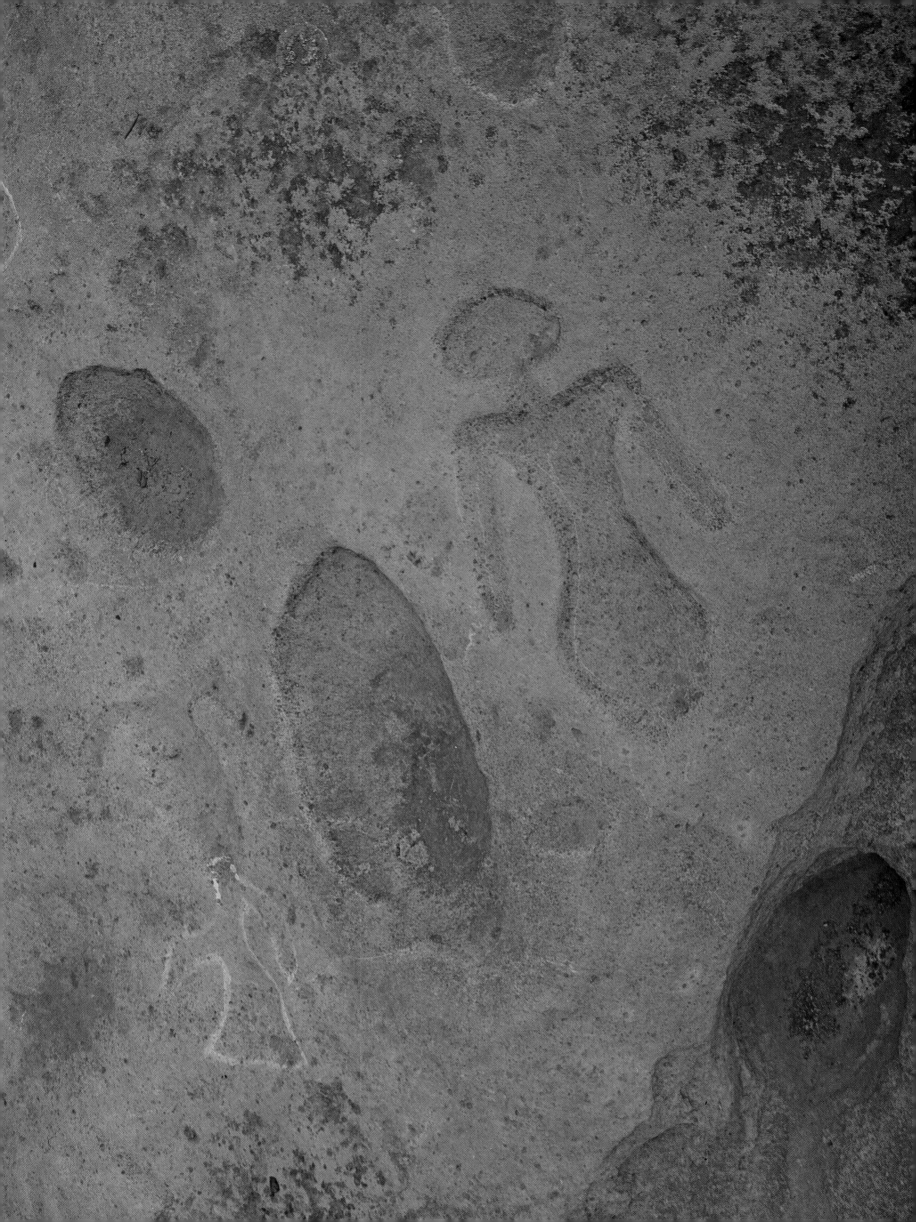

Above: Thousand Hills State Park, in the rolling hills of Adair County west of Kirksville, is one of Missouri's most beautiful. *Left:* Bollinger Mill was built in 1802 by Major George Frederick Bollinger on the Whitewater River. *Overleaf:* The hush of winter descends on Johnson Shut-Ins State Park on the East Fork of Black River, making it a remote place of solitude.

Above: The statue of Tom Sawyer and Huckleberry Finn in Hannibal honors Samuel Langhorne Clemens. *Right:* Falling Spring Mill, south of Winona in Oregon County, was built about 1860. *Overleaf:* Spring comes green against the blue haze of distant mountains in Belleview Valley along Highway 21 near Caledonia.

Above: Judge John Marshall Clemens built this house in Hannibal when his son, Samuel, was nine. The Clemens family lived in the house, described in *Tom Sawyer,* until 1853. *Left:* Pines blend into autumn hardwoods on Sutton Bluff, four miles northwest of Centerville in the Mark Twain National Forest.

Above: This red barn rises out of a field of soybeans in the rich farmland of Jackson County east of Kansas City. *Right:* The alluring waters of Round Spring flow from a circular sink beneath a natural bridge. The spring discharges up to 336 million gallons daily.

Above: The leaves of fragrant sumac add reds to autumn woods. Indians used sumac stems to make flutes. They made red dye and tea from the berries. *Left:* Alley Spring rises from a deep limestone basin and joins the Jacks Fork, now part of the Ozark National Scenic Riverways. Relatively heavy rainfall, and very porous limestone and dolomite rock create aquifers which are exposed by rivers resulting in Missouri's large concentration of springs.

Above: The Mississippi River flows south below Hannibal. Highway 79 from Hannibal south is called The Great River Road and provides many scenic views of the river. *Right:* Hickory, red cedar, and black oak feel winter beyond their autumn in the Huzzah State Forest and Wildlife Area in Crawford County.

Above: Once tallgrass prairie, the land north of the Missouri River near Vandalia is some of the state's richest farmland. *Left:* Leaves of the flowering dogwood are as beautiful in autumn as the flowers are in spring. *Overleaf:* Oaks and short-leaf pine surround Logger's Lake covered with water shield near Bunker.

Above: Pony Express riders carrying fifteen pounds of mail rode seventy-five miles a day over the 1,982-mile route between St. Joseph and Sacramento, California, in 1860-61. *Right:* The first permanent French settlement in Missouri was made at Ste. Genevieve about 1735. The Linden House suggests the beauty and strength of Missouri's first houses.

Above: Carefully tended rose gardens surround the entrance to the Albrecht Art Museum in St. Joseph. *Left:* Autumn is a special time in the Missouri Ozarks. Little Scotia Pond in the Mark Twain National Forest in Dent County is one of Missouri's many secluded places.

Above: The Missouri River near Hermann almost stands still on a late autumn evening. *Right:* Sycamores and willows shade a quiet, deep pool on the Meramec River.

Above: The Swan Lake Wildlife Area in Chariton County has nineteen hundred acres of water. Thousands of ducks and geese stop here during their north-south migrations each year. *Left:* Swirling water carved these 1.5 billion year old rhyolite rocks to form chutes, rapids, craters, and pools that are the Johnson Shut-Ins, considered among the most beautiful in America.

Above: Two fishermen cast their lines into the quiet dawn of the Lake of the Ozarks, a 55,500-acre lake with thirteen hundred miles of shoreline formed by damming the Osage River. *Right:* Beneath a bluff of dolomite, Blue Spring wells up from a depth of 250 feet and flows into Jacks Fork River three miles above Jam Up Cave.

Above: West from the Springbrook Wayside along Highway 63
north of Rolla, an infinity of spring greens reach for the horizon.
Left: Rich colors of autumn fill the flora of Mark Twain State Park
near Florida, where Samuel Clemens was born in 1835.

Above: Fertile farmland of the Osage River Valley lured early German immigrants to land near Westphalia. *Right:* The memoirs and historical papers of President Truman are preserved in the Harry S. Truman Library and Museum in Truman's hometown of Independence. *Overleaf:* Beyond Union Station, Kansas City's skyline rises from the south bank of the Missouri River.

Above: Ox-eye daisies bloom from May through August in meadows and fields throughout Missouri. *Left:* This waterwheel was once part of Turner Mill in the Irish Wilderness of Oregon County near the old townsite of Surprise. *Overleaf:* Daniel Boone found the Femme Osage valley while fur trapping in 1797. He returned to build this house in which he died in 1820.

Above: Tuam Sauk Mountain in Iron County boasts Missouri's highest elevation, 1,772 feet. The once-molten mountain rocks are more than a billion years old. *Right:* Wild sweet William blooms with May-apple of the barberry family and bloodroot of the poppy family, all found along streams and wooded slopes.

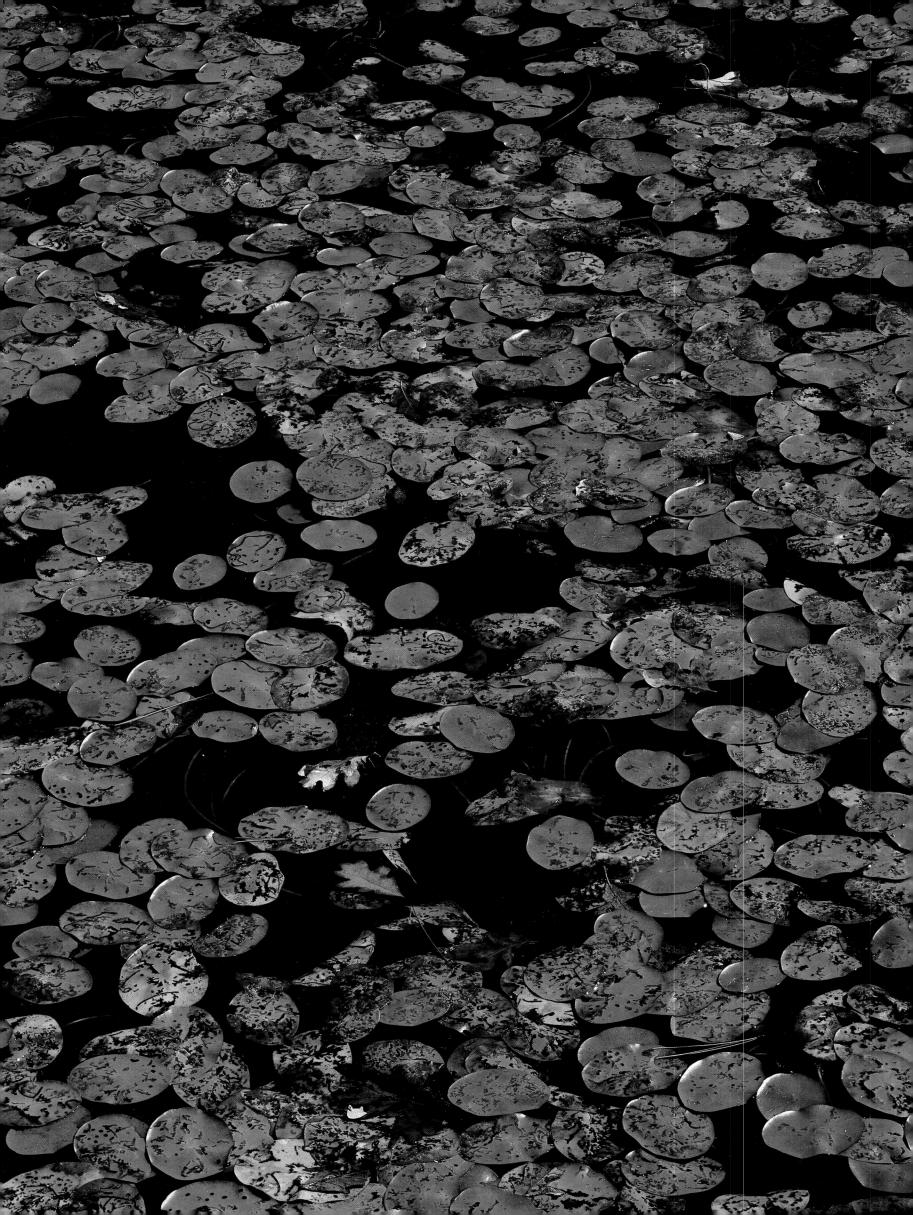

Above: Waters of Zanoni Spring in Ozark County near Gainesville once turned the overshot wheel of the Zanoni grist mill, now a place left quiet with the passage of time. *Left:* This water shield of the water-lily family covers much of Little Scotia Pond in Dent County.

Above: The Union Covered Bridge, built about 1870, spans Salt River in Monroe County near Paris. The 126-foot-long bridge is Missouri's last Burr-arch truss bridge. *Right:* Missouri has eight Blue Springs. This road leads to Blue Spring in the Meramec River basin of Crawford County. The rare curly-leafed muck-weed grows there.

Above: Jefferson Barracks was established in St. Louis on July 4, 1826. Col. Robert E. Lee and Lt. Ulysses S. Grant were stationed at this national historic site on the Mississippi River. *Left:* Karkhagne Scenic Drive runs from Highway 72 to Highway KK. The Karkhagne is a mythical, mischievous Ozark creature.

Missouri forests are filled once again with sturdy hardwoods. Greed, ambition, and lack of environmental awareness at the turn of the century had resulted in the plunder and waste of much of Missouri's timberland. The northern red oak in the foreground is one of nineteen species of oak trees growing in the state.

Above: The Jacks Fork, which flows into the Current from Texas and Shannon counties, is one of the wildest rivers in the state. *Overleaf:* The far horizon is Arkansas seen from the Sugar Camp Scenic Drive along the Missouri-Arkansas border in southwestern Missouri.

Above: The Ozark forest reclaims areas cleared by cutting or fire with new trees. Gum and locust trees are among the first hardwoods to turn color, usually in late summer. *Right:* Wild sweet William blooms in April through June in rich, rocky woods and often along streams. Its colors are corolla blue, purple, lilac, or rose-lavendar as seen here in the Irish Wilderness.

Above: St. Mary Aldermanbury Church, built in seventeenth-century London, was moved to and rebuilt at Westminster College in Fulton. Here Winston Churchill made his famous Iron Curtain speech in 1946. *Left:* The hawthorn, or red haw, is the official state flower. The hawthorn blooms throughout Missouri in April and May.

The Missouri River, more than one hundred miles longer than the Mississippi, gradually has become important for hydroelectric power and transportation. Here late afternoon sun warms poplars and cottonwoods near Rhineland.

The story told by the wind through Missouri grasses is an ancient
tale dating back as far as 500 million years when the seas receded
from the Ozark plateau for the last time.

Above: Corn and wheat are major Missouri crops that grow in rich farmland like this north of the Missouri River in Callaway County. *Right:* The flow from Greer Spring in Oregon County is Missouri's second largest with an average flow of 187 million gallons a day. Here the creek carries the water one quarter mile from the spring down to the Eleven Point River.

Above: From the air they look like thousands of earth's eyes full of sky. This farm pond looks into the sunset of Osage County near Westphalia. *Left:* If we only could hear the stories abandoned houses and barns like this one in Washington County might tell of the families who lived through winds and rains.

An elk browses in the woods of the 405-acre Lone Elk Park in southwestern St. Louis County where bison, elk, whitetailed and fallow deer, and Barbados sheep roam.

These mammoth granite boulders, called elephant rocks, are 1.2 billion years old and the main attraction at Elephant Rocks State Park in Iron County near Graniteville.

The magnificent world of Missouri's underground landscape can be found in caves like Onondaga Cave, one of Missouri's finest. Formed eons ago, these stalagtites hang up to fifty feet above the floor and are composed of calcium carbonate.

Above: Lake Jacomo, 970 acres of water in southeastern Jackson County, is a popular boating and fishing lake for people in the Kansas City metropolitan area. *Overleaf:* Weekend activities continue along the St. Louis riverfront well into morning. Viewed from Eads Bridge, city lights illuminate the Gateway Arch, Old Cathedral, and Busch Memorial Stadium.

One of Missouri's most scenic streams is the Current River. It carries the water of more springs than any other Missouri stream. This stretch is just above Cave Spring.

Earth, water, and sky fill with the beauty of sunset over the Duck Creek Wildlife Area north of Puxico. Duck Creek is a seasonal haven for migrating waterfowl and year round home for native birds and wildlife.

Above: The Current River and the Jacks Fork now are protected as part of the Ozark National Scenic Riverways. Below Paint Rock Bluff water shield borders another stretch of the Current River. *Right:* Moss, watercress, and dock grow in the 55-degree water of Cook Spring in Reynolds County.

Above: The tavern room and kitchen of this building at Old Missouri Town in Lake Jacomo Park east of Kansas City preserve the life style of Missouri's early settlers. *Left:* One of Missouri's most picturesque spring mills is the Alley Spring Mill, shown in the silence of ten degrees below zero. Alley Spring rises in Shannon County.

Above: Red Bluff on Huzzah Creek at the Davisville Campground in Crawford County shows the slow erosions of time and rains that draw the coloring of iron from ancient stone. *Right:* Flowering dogwood blooms in the Daniel Boone State Forest in Warren County, where small streams flow south five miles to join the Missouri River.

Above: The Liberty Memorial rises 217 feet above Kansas City, a tribute to those who served in World War I. *Left:* Water from Round Spring protects some of the watercress from winter ice in Round Spring Creek. *Overleaf:* The view is endless from vistas along the Scenic Drive near Big Spring in Carter County.

Kansas City is known as the City of Fountains. In addition, the lights beyond, outlining the buildings of Country Club Plaza, are an annual event between Thanksgiving and New Year's.

Above: Missouri's state capitol building, modeled after the nation's capitol, rises from the bluffs overlooking the Missouri River at Jefferson City. *Overleaf:* Glacial ice once leveled Northern Missouri, leaving behind rich soil. Some say the state will play a major role in feeding the world from farm fields like this one in Clay County northeast of Kansas City.

Above: Henry Shaw developed, endowed, and presented St. Louis with the Missouri Botanical Gardens, a place of incredible beauty where flowers bloom every day of the year. *Right:* Elegant textures and colors blend on a bluff above the East Fork of the Black River in Reynolds County.

Above: The Ionic columns, with Jesse Hall beyond, face Francis Quadrangle at the center of the University of Missouri/Columbia campus. *Left:* The magnificence of light, sky, and water are captured at Silver Mines Shut-In in Madison County near Fredericktown.

Above: The bluffs along the Missouri River, like these on the Lewis and Clark Trail near Bluffton, hold ancient tales of man and nature.
Right: Missouri forests call out, luring us deeper into the experience of the journey.